Chef John Lengseld

cooking with
Johnny Fish

cooking with
Johnny Fish

Seafood Appetizers
and
Entertaining Tips

chef john lengsfeld

PHOTOGRAPHY BY ROSANA BONILLA

MILL CITY PRESS

Mill City Press, Inc.
2301 Lucien Way #415
Maitland, FL 32751
407.339.4217
www.millcitypress.net

Printed in the United States of America

Paperback ISBN-13: 978-1-6322-1053-1
Ebook ISBN-13: 978-1-6322-1054-8

DEDICATION *and* ACKNOWLEDGEMENTS

I would like to thank some very special people that helped me keep my dream alive and supported me all these years

Ryan Hoope and Luis Antonio Pedro who graciously let me use their fabulous kitchen to prepare my dishes and their beautiful home to take photographs in.

My brother Chris and wife Jeanette Lengsfeld who assisted me when it came to doing all the meal planning, purchasing and executing of all the holiday meals.

Bobby Mills who graciously let me use his beautiful home to throw dinner parties take some awesome photos, and who spent many evenings keeping me calm while writing out the recipe slogans.

My mentor Desire Borges who took the time every day to remind me to live my life to the fullest, stay true to who I was and to never forget my dreams.

Matilda Miceli–The greatest friend anyone could ever ask for!

Chris and Amanda Clare and Brenden Clare for helping with my videos

My Wonderful parents Robert and Rita Audette who were there every step of the way with their support and encouragement.

And last but not least- **My Amazing Grandparents- Johnny and Connie Migliaccio** who are my angels.

All Italians know that when you have an Italian Mom, you are 100% Italian. Even though my Dad is German, that is how she raised us. I grew up on the Eastern part of Long Island with my brother Chris. My Maternal Grandparents lived about thirty minutes away. We saw them every weekend, we went there or they visited us. Like in most Italian homes, every Sunday was "Macaroni Day". We Neapolitans call it "Gravy" and we always ate dinner on Sunday between 1 and 2PM that was the rule. Mom left the food out just in case someone stopped over, was hungry, or wanted to pick on it later on. Growing up, I was very close to my Grandparents and spent all of my weeks off from school with them (holidays and most summer months)

I wasn't like other kids who would hang out at the arcade, in the mall or on the corner doing nothing. I loved being with my family. Now I know that all the time I spent with my Italian Grandparents gave me the best gift in life…LOVE! One of the things I had the privileging of learning was gardening. My Grandfather had a huge garden in a small yard and as a kid, it look like it went on for miles. I would help him turn up or rototill the ground, and then we would rake the entire area and get it ready for planting. He taught me how to place the seeds so they would have enough room to grow and how deep to plant them. During that time, I learned how to plant all kinds of fruits and vegetables, which included tomatoes (plum and beefsteak), squash (American and Italian), eggplant, string beans, Italian herbs and many more. Everything he taught me showed me how to care for the garden all through the summer, so we could yield a big harvest.

Grandpa and I always visited the farms on the Eastern end of Long Island. We did this every year at the end of summer so we could pick all of the tomatoes to jar them. Store bought tomatoes was never a thing. Hours would go by while we went up and down the farm collecting 8 to 12 bushels. The work was very hard, but I wouldn't trade that time I got to spend with him for any money. He was my Grandpa and this is what we did. After the farm, we would take the tomatoes home and leave them out on the table for a couple days to ripen (until we jarred them). These moments included some of the great things I learned which helped mold me as a person and ultimately as a chef.

As the years went on Grandpa (who was a butcher by trade) retired and always loved to fish, so of course he taught me how to, which became a love of mine too. With his boat, he would take my brother and me out almost every weekend. At the same time, he taught me how to bait and catch all different kinds of fish. We also went out for blue claw crabs and clamming, plain old fun. Around the age of 14, my Grandpa had a friend who owned a fish market close to their home and Grandpa would go there often to help them. At times he would bring me along and I felt like it was home just being around fish and all of those people. His friend noticed this and would let me help out by icing the fish and sweeping floors.

After a while, I would do anything just to be there. This store became so popular they opened a location across the street that was much bigger. At this point, I was turning 17 and going to a local college, but I really wanted to work at the fish store. Grandpa talked to his friend and I got a job working there while I was in college. This is when my culinary knowledge started to explode. I created different dishes that we could sell in the store for people to take home and heat up for dinner. All the dishes I created for the store made it into my journal because I had a dream that one day I would write a seafood cookbook.

And here we are…

THANK YOU for joining me in this exciting part of my life!
Johnny Fish

> *Make people feel like you're glad to have them there*

ENTERTAINING TIPS *for*
That PERFECT GATHERING

*H*aving people over doesn't have to induce a mild anxiety attack. Here, I break down 4 ways to prep for a party without blowing your cool; after all, the best host is one who actually enjoys their own party.

A few months ago, I hosted a dinner for friends that never really got off the ground. I couldn't understand it: I'd spent hours making a killer dishes I'd scrubbed and decluttered the apartment. I'd toiled over the music playlist.

Yet the whole evening was just kind of...blah. We all made chitchat, but it was a bit labored and punctuated by awkward silences. "I don't get it," I thought in a mild panic. "Why isn't this happening?" After my last guest made for the door—a few polite minutes after dessert—I was happy to proceed directly to my pajamas, relieved it was over.

Why do so many get-togethers leave us feeling vaguely unsatisfied and a little hollow? Because we focus a lot on entertaining—picking the perfect recipes, setting the right playlist—but don't really talk about the" how" of hosting once everyone is in the room. Throughout my book, I give tips on how to throw a successful party. But the cardinal rule for how to be a good party host is don't apologize about the lack of decorations or mention that you MEANT to have three more dishes, but only had time for two, or point out that your floor could have used a sweeping or five. No one wants to feel like the party or dinner or event is stressing you out.

sea scallops wrapped *in* prosciutto

These tasty treats can be for a cocktail party or a dinner with the family.
A different version of the commonly seen appetizer of scallops wrapped in bacon.
Using prosciutto allows for the subtle flavors of this meat to come through
without overpowering the wonderful flavor of the scallops.
Plump and juicy scallops sing along with an imported prosciutto
for a more sophisticated take on bacon-wrapped scallops.

Serves 4

INGREDIENTS:

8 jumbo sea scallops – whole pieces
Salt
Pepper
8 slices imported prosciutto

DIRECTIONS:

Preheat oven to 350 degrees.
Put a little salt and pepper onto the sea scallops
Wrap each one with a piece of prosciutto- if the piece is too big, cut it length wise- then wrap
Fasten with non-colored toothpicks.
Place on baking pan.
Bake for 15-20 minutes.
Place on platter and serve.

celery shrimp boats

Shrimp is always a crowd pleaser, and this appetizer, which combines it with tangy pineapple and tabasco, is no exception. Make up to a day in advance, if you like.

Serves 8 to 10

INGREDIENTS:

½ pound cooked salad shrimp 70/100 size
½ cup cream cheese
1 tablespoon lemon juice
⅓ cup crushed unsweetened pineapple
2 tablespoons walnuts, chopped
¼ teaspoon salt
2 teaspoon hot pepper sauce (Tabasco™)
3 large celery stalks, cut into 3-inch pieces
Dash paprika
1 tablespoon Mrs. Dash™ seasoning

DIRECTIONS:

Combine all ingredients in a large bowl except celery and paprika.
Fill celery with shrimp mixture.
Sprinkle with paprika.
Serve on one of your nicest platters.

clam fritters

Tasty and fun treat for any party or gathering.
Clam Fritters are a New England food, most commonly found in Rhode Island although they can also be found in Connecticut, Maine, and Massachusetts. They are deep-fried balls of battered clams. Here is JohnnyFish's version, which I'm sure you will just love.

Serves 4

INGREDIENTS:

1 6 1/2 ounce can chopped clams
3/4 cup all-purpose flour flour
1 teaspoon baking powder
1/2 teaspoon salt
1/2 teaspoon cayenne pepper
1 teaspoon black pepper
1/2 cup minced onion
1 large egg beaten
all-vegetable shortening
lemon wedges tartar sauce

DIRECTIONS:

Drain clams, reserving 1/4 cup juice.
Combine flour, baking powder, salt, cayenne pepper, and black pepper in a medium bowl.
Stir in clams and minced onion.
Combine clam juice and egg in a small bowl.
Add to flour mixture; stir until well blended.
Heat shortening to 365ºF in a deep saucepan or deep fryer.
Drop level tablespoons of clam mixture into the hot shortening. (Do not use fryer basket.)
Fry several fritters at a time for 3 1/2 minutes or until browned.
Drain on paper towels.
Serve with lemon wedges and
    tartar sauce.

johnny's pesto shrimp skewers

Homemade pesto with basil from my garden makes a scrumptious addition to shrimp. Serve these for dinner or make them at your next party.

Serves 4 to 6

INGREDIENTS:

1 ½ cups fresh basil leaves, chopped
3 cloves garlic
½ cup grated Parmigiano Reggiano
4 tablespoons olive oil
35 large shrimp, peeled and deveined
Kosher salt and fresh ground
   pepper to taste
7 wooden skewers

DIRECTIONS:

In a food processor, pulse basil, garlic, parmigiana reggiano cheese, salt and pepper until smooth.
Slowly add the olive oil while pulsing.
Combine raw shrimp with pesto and marinate a few hours in a bowl.
Soak wooden skewers in water at least 20 minutes (or use metal ones to avoid this step).
Thread 5 of the pesto marinated shrimp onto 7 skewers.
Heat an outdoor grill or indoor grill pan over medium low heat until hot. Be sure the grates are clean and spray lightly with oil.
Place the shrimp on the hot grill about 3-4 minutes, turn, and continue cooking about another 4 minutes.
Take them and serve on platter.

clam dip

This irresistible and super easy clam dip with cream cheese is a Johnny fish favorite and the perfect party appetizer, guaranteed to knock your socks off!

Yields 1 ½ cups

INGREDIENTS:

8-ounce cream cheese, softened
½ cup sour cream
1 ½ teaspoon lemon juice
Salt and pepper to taste
¾ teaspoon Worcestershire sauce
1 6 ½ ounces can minced
 clams, drained.

DIRECTIONS:

In a bowl, blend cream cheese and sour cream together well.
Stir in lemon juice, salt, pepper, and Worcestershire sauce.
Fold in minced clams into the mixture.
Chill and serve.

Johnny Options:
You can hollow out a loaf of pumpernickel bread to use as a bowl.

Gatherings need perimeters, or all the buzzy energy leaks out.

COMMIT *to a* SPECIFIC PURPOSE

*H*aving a clear intention for a party from the get-go will make your gathering less one size fits all or bland. Before you begin planning and event, ask yourself two questions.

"Why are we gathering?" and "Why is it important?"

Every time you reach a deeper reason, ask "Why" again.

Sometimes it takes four answers to get to the real objective. It's said that 90 percent of what makes a get-together successful is put in place before the event—starting with the space.

It's tempting to book a massive venue for your shindig, but bigger is not better.

One of my best friends Matthew Starnes who is a Full-service Wedding and Event planner at Hospitality Butler in North Carolina, always says the reason guests end up gravitating toward the kitchen, is that people instinctively seek out smaller spaces as the group dwindles, in order to maintain the density.

smoked salmon pinwheels

These elegant smoked salmon pinwheels are perfect if you want to enjoy lox without the bagels, for a low-carb, appetizer. I love smoked salmon, especially Nova Lox with cream cheese so this appetizer has my name all over it

Serves 10 to 12

INGREDIENTS:

8 ounces thinly sliced cold smoked salmon, I like Nova Lox

5 ounces cream cheese

½ medium cucumber, cut into matchsticks

3 tablespoons finely chopped red onion

2 tablespoons capers, drained

½ lemon, sliced thin

DIRECTIONS:

Lay a large piece of plastic wrap on a work surface.

Arrange the slices of salmon in an overlapping fashion to create a rectangle about 6 inches wide by 12 inches long, with one of the longest sides facing you.

Gently spread the cream cheese over the salmon trying not to break any of the pieces. Lay the cucumber along one side of the rectangle 1/2 inch from the edge.

Using the plastic wrap to guide you, roll the salmon up tightly around the cucumber sticks. Refrigerate until firm at least 30-35 minutes.

Using a sharp knife, cut the roll into 16 1/2-inch thick slices.

Sprinkle with red onion and capers and serve with lemon slices.

mexican crab dip

My Mexican crab Dip is zesty and is perfect for entertaining.
The spice level is totally customizable to your preferences.
Game Day, poolside, winter holidays; this dip will become a fast favorite!

INGREDIENTS:

1 pound imitation crab or 16 ounces pasteurized crabmeat, either one will work.
8 ounces lite cream cheese
1 cup salsa- I use medium hot
¼ cup finely chopped cilantro

DIRECTIONS:

Blend cream cheese until smooth.
Add salsa, cilantro, and crab.
Refrigerate overnight to allow flavors to blend.
Serve with crackers.

JOHNNY FISH TIP
for a healthier option, use
freshly cut vegetables
instead of chips

shrimp cocktail deviled eggs

YES! I love shrimp in pretty much anything, so I thought, "Why not put them on deviled eggs?" These make a wonderful appetizer for any get-together and are guaranteed to be a crowd-pleaser. I mean who doesn't love shrimp and deviled eggs!

Yield: 12 pieces

INGREDIENTS:

12 large size shrimp, peeled, deveined, and cooked (31-35 ct.)
6 large eggs, hard-boiled and peeled
2 ½ tablespoons mayonnaise
2 ½ tablespoons sour cream
2 teaspoons Dijon mustard
2 teaspoon fresh lemon juice
Salt and freshly ground black pepper
1/2 teaspoon Old Bay™ Seasoning

DIRECTIONS:

Halve eggs lengthwise.
Remove yolks and place in a small bowl.
Mash yolks with a fork, add mayonnaise, sour cream, mustard, Old Bay™, and lemon juice.
Add salt and pepper, to taste.
Fill egg whites evenly with yolk mixture.
Garnish with shrimp and make sure the shrimp is upright!
Add dill as a garnish if desired.
Store covered in the refrigerator
Chopped dill, optional

cheesy shrimp rounds

Who doesn't love shrimp, cheese, and more cheese?
Exactly, so this recipe fits the bill.

Serves 8-10

INGREDIENTS:

3⁄4 pound cooked shrimp,
coarsely chopped 8 ounces
  cream cheese,
softened 4 ounces of cheddar cheese
1 tablespoon lemon juice
2 tablespoons onion, minced
1 1⁄2 tablespoons horseradish
1⁄2 cup parsley, finely chopped
1⁄4 teaspoon salt

DIRECTIONS

Combine shrimp, onion, salt, cream cheese, cheddar cheese, lemon juice, and horseradish. Mix well.
With a tablespoon, scoop a quarter-size portion of the mixture and form into a ball. Roll each ball in chopped parsley. Refrigerate for 3 hours, then neatly place on a serving platter. Serve with crackers.

JOHNNY FISH TIP:
This recipe is great for a vegetable dip or spread.

scallop puffers

The scallops are great anytime of the year. My puffs are fun and can be used for that Holiday cocktail party or just for a family gathering.

Yields 36 puffs

INGREDIENTS:

3 tablespoons butter (salted)
¾ cup fresh scallops, finely chopped
  (Medium sea scallop is best)
½ cup fresh mushrooms,
  finely chopped
1 tablespoon grated onion
1 large clove garlic, peeled
  and crushed
¼ teaspoon fennel seeds, crushed
4 tablespoons flour
¼ cup whole milk
½ teaspoon dry mustard
2 teaspoon fresh lemon juice
1 ounce package frozen puff
  pastry, thawed.
Oil for frying (vegetable is best)

DIRECTIONS:

Melt butter in a large skillet.
Sauté scallops, mushrooms, onion
and garlic and fennel seeds for
2 minutes.
Stir in flour and continue cooking
until lightly brown.
Heat milk with mustard in a
small saucepan.
Pour onto scallop mixture.
Cook over medium heat, stirring
constantly until thick and smooth for
approximately 5 minutes.
Remove from heat, add lemon juice
and let cool.
Roll out pastry and cut into 36 rounds
using a 1 ¼ inch cookie cutter.
Roll each pastry circle out more until
very thin and almost transparent.
Place spoonful of scallop filling in
center of each pastry.
Fold over to form crescents–pinch
edges together (use beaten egg to
help seal them).
Fry puffs until golden brown.
Drain on paper towel. Serve

*S*tudies show that people disproportionately remember the beginning and the end of an experience. Yet we often pay the least amount of attention to how we open and close and event. We treat is as an afterthought and focus on the logistics and food instead. It's such a missed opportunity, starting and ending and event doesn't have to involve grand gestures or speeches. But I do suggest ushering people in by lighting a candle, pouring every guest a special drink at the same time, or making a brief welcome toast.

I had a Christmas party and I had guest send copies of two photos of happy moments from the past year. I decorated a Christmas tree with them, and after everyone arrived, they had a festive cocktail (that my bestie made) around the tree, sharing stories — starting the party on a personal, reflective note.

When I hosted an impromptu Friday night seafood dinner party, I made some brief remarks about why I felt moved to bring everyone together and me being a huge announcement type, I plunged right in and said the week we all just had was kind of sad because the news was particularly stressful and I said it was so reassuring to see their beautiful faces, which made me feel connected And grounded. And I was grateful that we could gather around the table on a relaxing night.

My friends all burst into applause.

connie's smoked salmon *and* asparagus spring bites

These little bites are always a crowd pleaser. I love them because they look impressive but are not very difficult to make. The only thing you have to be careful is not to overcook the asparagus, or it will lose its fresh green look

Serves 8 to 10

INGREDIENTS:

1 cup plain cream cheese, softened
½ cup finely chopped capers
2 tablespoons of lemon juice
2 ½ tablespoons finely chopped dill
10 spears of fresh asparagus,
  ends trimmed
1 large package of mini toasts (or
  you can use Melba Toast™)
Zest of one lemon
Freshly cracked black pepper
  (to taste)

DIRECTIONS:

Fill a large saucepan with water, add 1 tsp of salt, and place over medium-high heat. Bring to a boil.
Meanwhile, in a bowl, combine the cream cheese, capers, lemon juice and dill.
3Set aside for later.
Add ice to a large bowl of cold water, and place it next to your stove. You will need this to blanch the asparagus.

Add the asparagus to the boiling water.
Cook for about 3 minutes or until bright green and tender.
Use tongs to take the asparagus out of the boiling water and into the bowl of ice water. The asparagus will take about a minute to cool down, and then you can drain them. Once they are cool enough to handle, cut each spear into bite-sized pieces and set aside.
Find the serving tray or dish that you want to use, you will be assembling the canapés directly onto this dish.
Set out the toasts, and spread some of the cream cheese mixture on each one.
Next, wrap a piece of smoked salmon around each piece of asparagus. I just ripped the smoked salmon with my fingers; it doesn't have to be neat.
Place each salmon/asparagus bundle on top of the toasts, and top with the lemon zest and black pepper.

creole style johnnycakes

Serves 10 to 12

INGREDIENTS:

½ cup mayonnaise
1 large egg, beaten
2 tablespoon brown mustard
3 teaspoons Old Bay Seasoning™
2 teaspoons Garlic powder
1 teaspoon Cayenne pepper
2 tablespoons parsley, finely chopped
½ teaspoon salt
20 square saltine crackers
16 ounce can of jumbo lump crab
Breadcrumbs for dusting
Vegetable oil for frying
2 lemons cut up into wedges

DIRECTIONS:

Whisk together the first eight ingredients.
Crush the saltines and mix them in.
Very carefully fold in the crab lumps. Do this with your hands, it's so much easier.
Make into patties a little smaller than a hamburger.
Dust the tops of the cakes with the breadcrumbs, then put them on a sheet cookie sheet (or sheets) into the refrigerator and chill the cakes for about 20 minutes.
Put oil in a fry pan and cook the johnnycakes on both sides until brown.
Or if you prefer you can cook in the oven @ 350 until browned (about 30 minutes).
Get yourself a pretty platter and serve with lots of lemon wedges.

crab stuffed jalapenos

These are always a hit when I bring them to parties. They're especially great for sporting events and always seem to compliment the other food being served.

Serves 4-6

INGREDIENTS:

4 ounces fresh or canned
  lump crabmeat
3 ounces cream cheese softened
1 tablespoon of finely chopped
  fresh chives
1 teaspoon garlic powder
½ cup shredded Monterey
  Jack cheese
8 large Jalapenos, stemmed, half
  lengthwise and seeded
½ cup Panko breadcrumbs

DIRECTIONS:

Preheat oven to 400°
Stir together crabmeat, cream cheese, shredded cheese, chives, cilantro, and garlic powder.
Please have poppers on a foil lined baking sheet and gently stuff with crabmeat mixture.
Sprinkle breadcrumbs evenly over-stuffed peppers and bake until peppers are tender about 20 minutes at 350°
Broil until topping is golden brown approximately 2 to 3 minutes. Let cool slightly and serve.

lobster mushroom gondolas

These stuffed mushrooms take less than 20 minutes to whip up — but your dinner guests will never need to know that. Seriously, if you are looking for an easy, but impressive, lobster recipe, this is what you want to make.

Serves 6

INGREDIENTS:

1.5-pound cooked lobster meat chopped

1 cup condensed cream of mushroom soup- any brand will do

2 1/2 tablespoons breadcrumbs plain

2 tablespoons mayonnaise-Hellmann's™ or Dukes™

1/2 teaspoon Worcestershire sauce

1/2 teaspoon of black pepper

1/2 teaspoon of Tabasco™ sauce

24 mushroom caps about 1 1/2 inches in diameter stems removed

¾ cup of grated Italian Parmesan cheese

DIRECTIONS:

Preheat oven to 400°.

Combine lobster, soup, breadcrumbs, mayonnaise, Worcestershire and Tabasco™ sauce and pepper.

Stuff each mushroom with 1 hearty tablespoon lobster mixture.

Sprinkle with grated cheese

Place the mushrooms on a well-greased baking pan

Bake for 10 to 15 at 375 minutes or until lightly browned

Remove from oven and serve hot

mini crab cakes-*with a* spicy red pepper sauce

These succulent two-bite crab cakes are excellent as an appetizer especially with my spicy pepper sauce this appetizer will become one of your guest's favorites. Have them for a small dinner or for a cocktail party. Give each one a small dollop of the sauce just before serving. You can fry them up to 2 days ahead and refrigerate between layers of waxed paper; reheat in a 200°F oven on baking sheets.

INGREDIENTS:

1 pound- lump crabmeat-
  16 ounce can
4 green onions, thinly sliced
2/3 cup plain bread crumbs
1 1/2 teaspoon Old Bay™
  seafood seasoning
1 teaspoon ground black pepper
1 tablespoon Dijon mustard
1 egg
6 tablespoons mayonnaise, divided
1/4 cup chopped jarred roasted red
  bell pepper
2 teaspoons hot sauce
1 1/2 teaspoon lemon zest
1 tablespoon canola oil, more if needed

DIRECTIONS:

Place crabmeat in a large bowl and use your fingers to gently feel for and remove any pieces of shell or cartilage. Add green onions, breadcrumbs, seafood seasoning and pepper and toss to combine. In a small bowl, whisk together mustard, egg and 2 tablespoons of the mayonnaise and pour over the crab mixture.

Toss until combined, cover and refrigerate 30 minutes. Meanwhile, make the sauce. In a blender, combine bell pepper, hot sauce, zest and remaining 4 tablespoons mayonnaise; blend until smooth. Cover and refrigerate until ready to serve.

Form the crab mixture into 24 small cakes, each about 1 1/2 inches in diameter. Heat oil in a large nonstick skillet over medium heat. Working in batches, fry cakes until nicely browned and cooked through, about 3 minutes per side. Drain briefly on a paper-towel lined plate and serve warm with the pepper sauce.

RED PEPPER SAUCE

4 roasted red bell peppers, chopped
1 cup mayonnaise
2 tablespoon fresh tarragon, chopped
3 large garlic cloves, chopped
1 teaspoon Dijon mustard
½ teaspoon fresh lemon juice
½ teaspoon Tobacco™ sauce

SERVE ONE SPECIALTY COCKTAIL

Ask a Bestie to create a signature cocktail: *most of us have that fabulous friend or family member who just a-loves to get creative! Recruit them, and then brag about the drink on your invites! Little party details like fun straws can add a lot of fun and a pop of color.*

Also leave a Sharpie™ out for guests to label their glasses — you can wash it right off after the party. Clink, clink, clink. Yes, I have an announcement to make. You can write on your glassware with Sharpie™ and wash it off at the end of the night. Just draw and wipe it off with a paper towel when the party is over. You could also use dish soap, rubbing alcohol, or hand sanitizer. My mind = BLOWN...

rum glazed shrimp

These easy shrimps are an instant weeknight favorite.
Don't have a grill or grill pan? No worries! These will be just as delicious cooked in a skillet.

Serves 4

INGREDIENTS:
1 1/2-pound large size shrimp, peeled and deveined
3 tablespoons olive oil, divided
1/3 cup sweet chili sauce
1/4 cup soy sauce
1/4 cup Captain Morgan Spiced Rum™
2 cloves garlic, minced
Juice of 1 lime
½ teaspoon crushed pepper flakes
1 green onion, thinly sliced, for garnish

DIRECTIONS:
Place shrimp in a large bowl.
In a medium bowl, whisk together 2 tablespoons olive oil, sweet chili sauce, soy sauce, rum, garlic, lime juice, and red pepper flakes.
Add 3/4 of the marinade to the bowl of shrimp and let marinate in refrigerator for 15 to 30 minutes.
Heat remaining 1 tablespoon oil in a large pan or grill pan over medium-high heat.
Add shrimp and cook on one side until golden, about 2 minutes.
Using tongs, flip shrimp, then brush with remaining marinade.
Cook 1 to 2 minutes more.
Garnish with green onions and serve immediately.

grandpa johnny's famous baked clams

This is the best baked clams your ever gonna eat!
A Johnny Fish Favorite! And don't be chinsey with the garlic.
So much flavor packed into one bite, Grandpa Johnny's baked clams are tender
and sweet, the breading crispy, cheesy, zesty, garlicky, I could go on and on,
but let me show you how easy it is to make them.

Serves 4-6

INGREDIENTS:

2 dozen top Neck clams – medium size
1 ½ cup Italian breadcrumbs
2 tablespoons grated Pecorino Romano cheese
4 cloves garlic, chopped or 5
3 tablespoons fresh parsley, chopped
1 teaspoon dried basil
1 teaspoon dried oregano
5 tablespoons extra virgin olive oil
Salt & pepper

DIRECTIONS:

Wash the clams under fresh water, shuck them and leave the clam on the half shell.
In a bowl, add your ingredients and mix well until the oil has been fully absorbed by the breadcrumbs. The bread will look uniformly wet.
Add salt and pepper as desired.
Place all the open clams in a baking sheet and with a teaspoon put the breadcrumb mixture in each clam until the clam is completely covered.
Bake at 375 for 12-15 minutes, then put under the broiler for 1 minute to brown.
Watch them so they don't burn

fried calamari ala johnny fish

How do you make fried calamari? I'm gonna tell you how! My calamari is the Best!
The first step in this recipe is to marinate the squid in buttermilk. Mix together flour and seasonings to create the coating for the squid. Dredge the calamari in the seasoned flour, then place it in a pot of hot oil to cook. Drain, then serve immediately with your choice.
Breading: If you prefer a crunchier coating, add 1/4 cup of cornmeal or seasoned breadcrumbs to the flour mixture. I'm gonna give you a hint that I learned many years ago and that it is to par boil the squid for like 2 minutes- That takes the water out of the squid so it cooks nice and even!!!! Ehhyyy forget bout It!!

Serves 6

INGREDIENTS:

2 pounds calamari rings and
   tentacles- you can get these frozen
   at any market
1 cup buttermilk
2 cups all-purpose flour
2 teaspoons salt plus more
   for serving
2 teaspoons paprika smoked
   or regular
1/4 teaspoon pepper
1 teaspoon garlic powder
Vegetable oil for frying
Teaspoons chopped fresh parsley

DIRECTIONS:

Seasonings: While I typically stick with a mix of paprika, salt, pepper and garlic powder, you can add other seasonings such as cayenne pepper, onion powder, Italian seasoning, dried parsley, or Old Bay™ seasoning.

Place the calamari in a bowl with the buttermilk and stir to combine.
Cover the bowl and refrigerate for at least 30 minutes.
Heat 3-4 inches of oil in a large deep pot to 375 degrees F.
Place the flour, salt, paprika, pepper and garlic powder in a medium bowl; stir to combine.
Remove each piece of squid from the buttermilk and dredge in the flour. Repeat the process until all pieces are coated. I use a fork so your hands sticky free Place 8-10 pieces of squid in the oil.
Cook for 2-3 minutes or until golden brown.
Remove the squid from the oil and drain on paper towels. Repeat the process with

johnny's street fish tacos bites

My version of the street fish taco is always a hit at parties,
Fun and delicious and you can't stop at just one.

Serves 4

INGREDIENTS:

1/2 cup salsa Verde- available in any
   supermarket
4 ounces cream cheese, softened
2 tablespoons lime juice, divided
3 tablespoons minced fresh cilantro
2 teaspoon honey
Dash salt
36 large cooked shrimp
2 tablespoon taco seasoning
36 tortilla chip scoops
1-1/2 cups coleslaw mix
3/4 cup cubed avocado
3/4 cup chopped seeded tomato
Lime wedges and additional minced
   fresh cilantro

DIRECTIONS:

In a blender, combine the salsa,
cream cheese, 1 tablespoon lime juice,
cilantro, honey and salt.
Cover and process until smooth;
set aside.
Put the cooked shrimp in a
bowl and sprinkle with the taco
seasoning and mix.
Meanwhile, place tortilla chips on a
serving platter.
In a small bowl, combine the
coleslaw mix, avocado, tomato,
remaining lime juice and 1/2 cup
salsa mixture.
Spoon into chips.
Place a cooked shrimp in each chip;
top each with about 1/2 teaspoon
salsa mixture. Garnish with lime
wedges and additional cilantro.

tuna topper turnovers

Say that 5 times fast! As fun as it is to say, it is even more fun to make and eat.

Makes 24 turnovers

INGREDIENTS:

1 tablespoon chopped onion
1 4oz can mushrooms, drained, reserve liquid
½ cup chopped pitted green olives
2 tablespoons butter
1 teaspoon flour
1 large clove garlic, peeled and crushed
¼ teaspoon salt
2 6 ½ oz. can tuna white fish, drained
2 pastry piecrusts (not preformed)

DIRECTIONS:

In a saucepan, sauté onion, mushrooms, and olives in butter for 5 minutes.
Stir in flour, garlic, salt and reserved mushroom liquid.
Heat thoroughly.
Add tuna and mix well.
Remove from heat.
Preheat oven to 450 degrees.
Roll out pastry. Cut into 2 ½ inch circles (use cookie cutter).
Place 2 teaspoons of tuna mixture in the center of each pastry.
Fold over pastry. Moisten to seal (water or beaten egg).
Place tuna toppers on baking sheet.
Bake for 6-7 minutes or until crust is golden brown.
Remove, place on serving platter.

HAVE GOOD MUSIC PLAYING...*Always*!

There's nothing that kills a party more than silence. Now that there are music apps like Spotify, Radio, iTunes Radio, Alexa and Google Play Music (even your TV, with endless music channels and apps), it's easy to set the perfect tone and energy for any occasion. A little secret: The reason my food comes out so good is I play Italian music while I cook. True story.

blue cheese stuffed jumbo shrimp

What's not to love about jumbo shrimp stuffed with creamy, delicious blue cheese?
I mean come on… That's the life!

Serves 4

INGREDIENTS:

3 ounces cream cheese, softened
2/3 cup minced fresh
  parsley, divided
1/4 cup crumbled blue cheese
1 teaspoon chopped shallot
1/2 teaspoon Dijon mustard
24 cooked jumbo shrimp, peeled
  and deveined

DIRECTIONS:

In a small bowl, beat cream cheese
until smooth.
Beat in 1/3 cup parsley, blue cheese,
shallot and mustard.
Refrigerate at least 1 hour.
Make a deep slit along the back of
each shrimp to within 1/4-1/2 in. of
the bottom.
Stuff with cream cheese mixture;
press remaining parsley onto cream
cheese mixture.

crab bites *with a* lemon garlic dipping sauce

These appetizer bites are a FUN way to enjoy crab for your next gathering. Crab, fresh parsley and spices are folded into breadcrumbs, shaped and lightly fried for the perfect bite. Serve with lemon-garlic sauce for dipping. Can it get any better, I don't think so.

Yields 35 balls

INGREDIENTS:
1 pound lump crabmeat, flaked
¼ cup butter, melted
1 teaspoon salt
⅛ teaspoon cayenne pepper
1 teaspoon dry mustard

1 ½ teaspoon fresh parsley chopped
2 teaspoon Worcestershire sauce
1 cup Italian breadcrumbs
2 egg yolks, lightly beaten
½ cup flour
Oil for frying

DIRECTIONS:
Place crabmeat in a mixing bowl.
Add butter, salt, cayenne pepper, mustard, parsley flakes, Worcestershire sauce, breadcrumbs, and egg yolks to crab.
Mix well.
Refrigerate 2-3 hours or until stiff enough to handle.
Form crab mixture into 35 walnut-sized balls.
Roll over flour.
Heat oil to 360 degrees in a heavy saucepan.
Fry balls until golden brown.

LEMON GARLIC SAUCE
1 cup mayonnaise
2 teaspoons Dijon mustard™
1 teaspoon finely chopped garlic
2 teaspoons fresh lemon juice
¼ teaspoon salt

johnny's rockin oysters rockefeller

This is a slight variation on the classic dish Oysters Rockefeller. Serve this delicious dish and watch your guests cry, 'I love you Johnny Fish'

Serves 6

INGREDIENTS:

36 oysters on the half shell
2 cups cooked spinach
1/2 cup chopped yellow onion
6 sprigs of flat (Italian) parsley
1 teaspoon celery salt
½ teaspoon salt
Eight drops Tabasco sauce
7 tablespoons of butter unsalted
3/4 cup Italian breadcrumbs
1/4 cup of grated Parmesan cheese

DIRECTIONS:

Preheat oven to 400°
Please oysters on baking sheet
Put spinach, onion, parsley through a food processor or chopped finally with a knife add the celery salt, salt and Tabasco sauce.
Melt butter in a skillet, cook spinach mixture for five minutes, add breadcrumbs and mix well
Sprinkle spinach mixture over oysters and bake for 10 minutes remove from oven and serve hot.

mac *and* cheese crab minis

These cheesy minis are so cheesy; with delicious crabmeat,
it makes an elegant twist that makes them the perfect party appetizer!

Yields 36-40 bites serves 12 to 15

INGREDIENTS:

1-pound mini elbow pasta
½ cup panko breadcrumbs- you can
   use Italian flavored
2 tablespoons salted butter
2 tablespoons all-purpose flour
Pinch of nutmeg
1/2 teaspoon pepper
1/2 teaspoon salt
1 1/4 cups whole milk- or 2%
2.1/2 cups grated parmigiana cheese
5 ounces lump crabmeat

DIRECTIONS:

Preheat oven to 400°F.
Bring a large pot of water to a boil,
add pasta and cook until al dente,
about 7 minutes.
Drain well
Spray 36 mini muffin
cups with PAM,
Sprinkle the bottom of each muffin
cup with a small amount of panko.

In a large saucepan, melt the butter
over medium heat.
Whisk in flour and cook for
2 minutes.
Add nutmeg, salt and pepper and
whisk until combined.
Whisk in the milk and cook until
small bubbles form at the edges of
the pan; about 5 minutes.
Remove pan from heat and add
the cheese, stirring constantly
until smooth.
Add the pasta and crab; stir until
coated with the cheese sauce.
Using a small dough scoop add about
a tablespoon of the mixture to each
muffin cup.
Bake for 20 minutes or until the
edges of the pasta begin to turn
golden brown. Remove from oven
and cool for 10 minutes.
Carefully remove each bite from the
muffin tin and serve immediately.

johnny's new york style lobster heroes
Cause in New York we do it right!

INGREDIENTS:

1 pound cooked lobster meat- cut into bite sized chunks
½ cup mayonnaise extra thick Hellman's™ for this one
3 teaspoons fresh lemon juice
½ cup chopped celery
1/3 cup green tops of the scallions chopped
A few dashes of Tabasco™ if you like it hot add more dashes
Pinch of salt
2 pinches of black pepper
Split hero loafs 3 or 4
3 tablespoons of melted unsalted butter

DIRECTIONS:

Place the cooked lobster meat in large bowl.

In a separate, smaller bowl combine the mayonnaise, lemon juice, celery, parsley, scallion, hot sauce, and salt and pepper.

Mix and taste for seasoning.

Once you have the seasoning to your liking, add to the cooked lobster meat and mix.

Brush both sides of rolls with butter and toast both sides in a medium fry pan over medium heat until nicely browned.

Divide the lobster salad between each roll per your preference.

Some serve this with shredded lettuce under the lobster salad but I don't, you can.

A host's primary duty isn't to feed people (really!) but to spend time with them.

ALWAYS *Be* PRESENT

E *ach time you get up to get something; you essentially abandon your guests. Serve family-style, which many of my seafood appetizers recipes are and forget cleaning up mid event. Carrying plates to the kitchen is one thing; but once you turn on a tap, you've doused the festivity and believe me maybe two of your friends will help you*

bob *and* rita's steamed littleneck clams
with a butter garlic sauce

It's always nice to have a quick, easy and delicious seafood recipe on hand and my parents Bob and Rita do it right! What I love about this recipe is that you can serve these clams as an appetizer or serve them over a bed of pasta for a meal. A win-win situation here!

INGREDIENTS:

3 dozen Littleneck clams
2 sticks of salted butter, divided
8 cloves of garlic, freshly minced
1 cup Chardonnay, choose a buttery Chardonnay
2 tablespoons lemon juice, freshly squeezed
3 tablespoons Italian parsley, finely chopped
1 lemon, cut into wedges, for garnish

DIRECTIONS:

In a large heavy sauté pan, melt 3 tablespoons of the butter.
Add garlic and sauté for 30-40 seconds until the garlic smells fragrant.
Add wine and lemon juice and bring to a boil
Add clams and the remaining butter.
Cover with lid
Steam for about 8 minutes.
Check to make sure your clams have opened.
Remove from heat and discard any unopened clams
Sprinkle with 1 tablespoon of parsley
Transfer to a large bowl or serve in the sauté pan
Serve with lemon wedges and extra 1 tablespoon of parsley on the side.

salmon croquettes
with remoulade dipping sauce

Salmon Croquettes sound so funny, but they are super easy to make! Big chunks of salmon are combined with breadcrumbs, herbs and seasonings and formed into patties. Deliciously crispy on the outside and flavorful on the inside… one of my favorites!

Serves 6

INGREDIENTS:

Remoulade:
2 cups mayonnaise
1 tablespoon capers
3 teaspoons Old Bay™
3 teaspoons crushed garlic
3 teaspoons lemon juice
3 green onions (scallions),
  finely chopped

CROQUETTES:

2 pre-cooked salmon fillets,
  about ½ pound
1 egg, lightly beaten
1 cup fish fry coating mix, plus more
  for coating (any brand will do)
8 dashes of hot sauce
¼ cup remoulade sauce, recipe above
Canola oil for frying

DIRECTIONS:

For Remoulade
Combine all the remoulade ingredients, except the scallions, in a bowl.
Stir together with a fork to help break up the capers.
Mix in scallions and set aside.
For Croquettes
Using a fork, flake the salmon meat away from the skin.
Throw out the skin.
In a medium bowl, beat egg.
To the egg, add the fish fry mix, salmon, hot sauce and ¼ cup of remoulade sauce.
Mix well to combine.
Form into 8 patties.
Pour the remaining fish fry mix into a pie dish or onto a dish.
Coat the patties in the remaining fish fry mix and set aside.
In a large pan, heat a thin layer of oil over medium to medium high heat.
Without crowding pan, cook patties until golden brown, about 3 to 4 minutes per side.
Serve Croquettes hot with remaining remoulade sauce.

italian style mussels *ala* bianco

These Tasty mussels are so full of flavor, I serve them at every dinner party I have, and my guests go wild over them. When they eat them they yell we love you Johnny!

Serves 4

INGREDIENTS:

5 tablespoons extra virgin olive oil
2 shallots, finely chopped
5 garlic cloves, finely chopped
2 ½ pounds mussels, cleaned (Prince Edward Island Mussels are the best for this).
1 ½ cup dry white wine
½ bunch fresh parsley, chopped
Kosher Salt
Crusty Italian bread to serve

DIRECTIONS:

Heat the olive oil in a large pot over medium heat.
Add the shallots and garlic and cook until softened, about 5 minutes.
Add the mussels, wine, parsley and season well with salt.
Give it a good stir, cover the pot, cook until mussels open, and are cooked through, about 10-12 minutes.
Serve with the crusty bread.

johnny's seafood platter

This cold fish platter is always a crowd pleaser.
Make your party come alive with this array of shellfish.

Serves 6

INGREDIENTS:
Crushed Ice
Green kale bunches
1 cooked Maine lobster
Beautiful platter
5 pounds cooked jumbo shrimp,
 peeled and deveined, with tails on
 26/30 count
6 Lemons, halved
Mustard Sauce or Cocktail Sauce,
 recipes follow

MUSTARD SAUCE INGREDIENTS:
1 1/2 cups good mayonnaise
3 tablespoons Dijon mustard
1 1/2 tablespoon whole
 grain mustard
¼ teaspoon kosher salt

COCKTAIL SAUCE INGREDIENTS:
1 cup ketchup (Heinz™ is the best)
1 ½ tablespoons fresh lemon juice
1 tablespoon Worcestershire sauce

2 tablespoons prepared horseradish
2 cloves garlic, minced
4 dashes Tabasco™ sauce
½ teaspoon white pepper

DIRECTIONS:
For Mustard Sauce
Mix all ingredients together.

For Cocktail Sauce
Mix the ketchup, lemon juice,
Worcestershire sauce and garlic in a
small bowl.
Add 1 tablespoon of horseradish,
taste, add more if desired.
Then stir in a few dashes of hot sauce
if you like your cocktail sauce with
an extra kick.

For Seafood Platter
Fill a large platter with crushed ice.
Place the seafood and lemons artfully
on top of the ice.
Serve with the sauces.

*end with a
personal touch by
walking each guest
to the door*

CLOSE YOUR EVENT DECISIVELY

*W*e've all been there: Its late, people are furtively tiptoeing toward the door, and the party fizzles out. Guests want structure and direction, —so signal the end with an exit line. Make a speech, Thank everyone and wrap up with a few highlights from the event. If you're hosting at your home, suggest that everyone move to the living room for "one last" drink or coffee.

Then end with a personal touch by walking each guest to the door to say goodbye. Prolong the warmth by handing them a small keepsake or treat as they head out. After my seafood dinner party, I brought out a bowl of fancy chocolate bars and had every guest choose one. I watched in amusement as my friends, solidly in midlife, acted like greedy toddlers, playfully squabbling over their favorites. My friends still talk about that bowl of candy bars. These are tiny little acts, but they add up to something bigger. They say, 'You matter.'"

Lastly the one thing you should do to make any party or event is successful is to *spend time with the people you love!*

CONTACT INFO

John@cookingwithjohnnyfish.com
My email address

Cookingwithjohnnfish.com
Website

Cooking with JohnnyFish
Facebook

cooking_with_johnnyfish
Instagram

Cooking with JohnnyFish
Linkedin
https://www.linkedin.com/company/cooking-with-johnnyfish

Corporate office number of JohnnyFish
407.209.4601

CPSIA information can be obtained
at www.ICGtesting.com
Printed in the USA
LVHW070819021120
670441LV00018B/462